Remembering Things

A play

Michael Fosbrook

Samuel French—London
New York-Toronto-Hollywood

REMEMBERING THINGS

First presented at the Perton Centre, Perton, near Wolverhampton, on 29th October, 1999, with the following cast:

Mrs Weston	Jane Fosbrook
Rosemary	Sara Plant
Derek	John Campbell

Directed by Michael Fosbrook

CHARACTERS

Mrs Weston; a widow, in her late seventies or early eighties
Rosemary; a uniformed policewoman, twenty-four
Derek; a detective constable, about thirty

The action takes place in the front room of Mrs Weston's house

Time — the present

Also by Michael Fosbrook
published by Samuel French Ltd:

Figuring Things

REMEMBERING THINGS

The front room of Mrs Weston's house

Although Mrs Weston is far from well-to-do, the room and furniture look clean, respectable, and well cared for. In the room are a table and chairs; otherwise the setting is as simple as required

When the play begins Rosemary, a uniformed policewoman of twenty-four, and Mrs Weston, a widow in her late seventies or early eighties, are sitting at the table. Mrs Weston is staring into space. Rosemary is trying to attract her attention

Rosemary Mrs Weston? (*She pauses slightly*) Mrs Weston — can you hear me?

Mrs Weston Eh?

Rosemary You didn't seem to be —

Mrs Weston (*sharply*) I'm not deaf. Not everybody my age is decrepit.

Rosemary (*finding Mrs Weston's abruptness comical, despite herself*) I'm sorry. I didn't mean to ——

Mrs Weston Amuse you, do I?

Rosemary No — of course you don't. I was only trying to ——

Mrs Weston In a hurry?

Rosemary We can take as long as you need, Mrs Weston.

Mrs Weston That police policy, is it?

Rosemary We don't want to rush you.

Mrs Weston I'd have thought you'd have been in a hurry. Most people are these days. And there's enough crime, isn't there?

Rosemary There certainly is.

Mrs Weston Do *you* live on your own, dearie? (*She looks hard at Rosemary*)

Rosemary No … (*Intimidated into elaboration*) No, I share a house. With a friend.

Mrs Weston Man friend, is he?

Rosemary Mrs Weston, if you don't mind, I think we ought to get down to business.

Mrs Weston Business?

Rosemary I mean, we ought to try to find out ——

Mrs Weston You are in a hurry then, aren't you? (*She pauses slightly*) Well, is he?

Rosemary Is he what?

Mrs Weston Your man friend.

Rosemary Yes.

Mrs Weston I have the telly on as loud as you can, every night.

Rosemary (*lost*) Oh.

Mrs Weston I don't think as it would scare them off, really. All it does is give me a bloody headache.

Rosemary Yes — I imagine it would.

Mrs Weston Did you see in the paper? That woman in Arleton. Eighty-two, she were. Older than me. All them bruises round her eyes. Well, the one was closed. And stitches. Looked like Frankenstein. And Arleton's a posh area, you don't think as that sort of thing ——

Rosemary You weren't attacked, were you, Mrs Weston?

Mrs Weston She let him in. The one who went for her. That's what makes it so frightening. She let him in. She must have known him, see. And she let him in.

A slight pause

Rosemary I know that poor woman had a terrible experience. And I know what happened to her is very frightening to — to someone like yourself. Believe me, I do understand, Mrs Weston. But we need to try to sort out what happened to you this ——

Mrs Weston How old are you?

Rosemary Twenty-four.

Mrs Weston I thought so. You haven't got much to remember. When you're older you'll … How long do you think I've had these slippers?

Rosemary Well, I couldn't really ——

Mrs Weston Ten years. And Charlie had 'em afore that.
Rosemary Charlie?
Mrs Weston They're still the best slippers as I've ever had.
Rosemary Was Charlie your husband?
Mrs Weston Well, I wasn't talking about the Prince of bloody Wales.

Pause

Rosemary Mrs Weston, I do have to ask a few questions, if you don't mind. Can you please tell me where the money was taken from?
Mrs Weston The kitchen. That's usually where you keep a tea caddy, ain't it?

Rosemary gets up and heads for the kitchen

Rosemary Right. I wonder if we could just take a ——
Mrs Weston Where you going?
Rosemary It would be helpful to have a look in your kitchen.
Mrs Weston What for? There's nothing to see. It's gone.
Rosemary I know the money's missing, but ——
Mrs Weston Not much point in looking for summat as isn't there.
Rosemary I need to have a look at what we call — the scene of the crime.
Mrs Weston Oh, yes? And what do I call it?
Rosemary Mrs Weston — you do want us to find out who took your money, don't you?
Mrs Weston There's no need for you to do that.
Rosemary But if you've had a large sum of money taken, you must want the person who took it to be found and ——
Mrs Weston I know who took it.

Pause

Rosemary You know who took it?
Mrs Weston I just told you.

Rosemary When my sergeant sent me here, he didn't mention
that ——
Mrs Weston My daughter and her husband took it.

A slight pause

Rosemary Your daughter and your son-in-law?
Mrs Weston Leastways, I know it was Clifford. I can't believe as
it was Annie.
Rosemary How do you know ——
Mrs Weston My own daughter. Can you believe it?
Rosemary How do you know that they took your money, Mrs
Weston?
Mrs Weston Because it's gone. If they hadn't took it, it'd still be
there.
Rosemary What I meant was, how do you know it was them as
opposed to anyone else?
Mrs Weston Who else has been here?
Rosemary So your daughter and son-in-law were here earlier this
morning, were they?
Mrs Weston No.
Rosemary Mrs Weston, I'm having great difficulty understanding
exactly what ——
Mrs Weston You don't learn nowt if you scream and shout.

Pause

Rosemary Perhaps you could tell me everything that happened in
your own words. That might be easier than me asking questions
all the time.
Mrs Weston You remind me of my Maureen.
Rosemary Is Maureen your daughter?
Mrs Weston Yes.
Rosemary And you think she stole your money?
Mrs Weston No.

A slight pause

Rosemary Mrs Weston, I thought you just said ——

Mrs Weston I was talking about Annie. You didn't listen.

Rosemary I'm sorry. You did mention ——

Mrs Weston Maureen's the one who lives in Leicester. Too far to come and see me, but always puts on her posh voice on the phone. You'd think her phone was out in the street, where all the neighbours can hear her.

Rosemary (*getting back to the subject*) So the one you suspect is Annie?

Mrs Weston I don't suspect. I know. I know her. And Clifford. I know what they did.

Rosemary Clifford is her husband?

Mrs Weston Stop interrupting, and I'll tell you. *(She pauses slightly)*

During the following, Rosemary produces a notebook and pen and tries to take notes

Annie and Clifford come round yesterday afternoon. They come most Saturdays. Clifford don't normally stay, he's off to his allotment. Half the time he only sits in that shed smoking his pipe. One chap has got a portable telly down there. Runs it off a car battery. I think Annie's glad to be rid of him. She comes for a bit of peace. He has a stubborn streak in him. Always has had. I'm sure he encouraged their Gail to get them tattoos ——

Rosemary So Annie and Clifford came round yesterday afternoon?

A slight pause

Mrs Weston They say as they do odd jobs for me. Think I can't look after meself. I spend all afternoon making tea and tidying up after them. They think they mean well. Clifford chucks cigarette ends in my flowerbeds.

A slight pause

Rosemary So — you made them lots of tea, and Clifford made lots of mess.

Mrs Weston I know what you want, dearie. You think I find this easy?

Rosemary No, I don't suppose ——

Mrs Weston I've got three grandchildren by Annie.

Rosemary I am sorry, Mrs Weston. I know how difficult this must be.

Mrs Weston You don't. You let me go, and I'll get there. (*She pauses slightly, then gets up*) I said to Clifford, I said, "Clifford, you're a big chap, you reach me down that tea caddy." He knows I like to check it, see. I don't know why I asked him, I usually stand on a chair, but he needs summat to do. They was both sat there, drinking tea. And they say, you should put your money somewhere else. A tea caddy is for tea, not money, they says. "Five pound notes don't make a very nice cuppa," says Clifford. He was pretending to joke. "Six hundred pound is a lot to have in the house," they say. "Your life savings." And what do they know? I can't get to no bank. And they're eyeing that money all the time. I know they are. They're pretending not to look at it, and they're being all concerned about me. They don't care, I know they don't. Annie wants a new cooker. And Clifford would spend a fortune on that allotment, given the chance. They was looking at it all the time. Even when their eyes was on the ceiling or in their tea-cups they was looking at it. Clifford couldn't get his pipe going properly, and Annie was sitting still. She's hardly ever still, she's usually fidgety and moving about. I knew they was looking at it, and they kept on looking. They couldn't stop. That was why I never got the money out, just to show I knew they was looking, and Clifford said he'd give me a lift to a bank or a building society any time. His eyes were on the wall, but he were looking at the money. And they kept looking and looking. They was looking all the time. (*She pauses*) They took it when the phone rang. It's in the hall, see. I had to go and answer it. I don't let no-one else answer the phone in my house. When I come back, Clifford looked at Annie and said, "Don't stretch yourself, Ma, I'll put it back for you". They was looking at each other. Can you imagine it? Your own flesh and blood. Annie didn't say nothing. She was reading the paper. Clifford put the caddy back. He didn't say nothing. And he didn't say nothing for the next five minutes, though you can't usually get him to stop gassing about this and that. Then they upped and left, really quiet. I should have checked it straight away. I could see what they was thinking. But it wasn't till just now as I thought to look at it again. I should have checked it before. Can you believe it, though? I'd let 'em in any time. They're flesh and blood. Well, Annie is. Stealing from your own mother. I'd never have thought it. Could you do that? Could you?

Rosemary No, Mrs Weston, I don't think I could.

Mrs Weston (*sitting again*) What happens now?

Rosemary We shall have to interview your daughter and son-in-law.

Mrs Weston To arrest them?

Rosemary They have to have the chance to present their own version of events.

Mrs Weston Lies, you mean.

Rosemary We have to consider all the evidence.

Mrs Weston My word against theirs, you mean?

Rosemary Perhaps.

Mrs Weston So there isn't any.

Rosemary Evidence? There might be.

Mrs Weston I had my hair done on Friday. D'you like it?

Rosemary Yes — it's very nice.

Mrs Weston D'you really think so?

Rosemary It suits you very well.

Mrs Weston Can I ask you something, er — what's your name?

Rosemary Rosemary.

Mrs Weston Are you an honest person, Rosemary? Do you tell the truth?

Rosemary Most of the time.

Mrs Weston If you tell Annie and Clifford I know as they took my money, will it do me any good?

Rosemary Only you can answer that, Mrs Weston.

Mrs Weston Would they still come and see me?

Rosemary Would you want them to?

Mrs Weston Yes. (*A slight pause*) Sometimes you're best off not telling the truth.

Rosemary Sometimes. But only over small things.

Mrs Weston Like hairdos.

Rosemary Like hairdos. But not robbery. And as you said — who else could have done it?

Mrs Weston I could've left the back door open. I've done it before. Clifford will tell you that. (A *slight pause*) I want you to drop it. Forget it.

Rosemary Is that what you really want?

Mrs Weston It isn't what I want. You know it isn't what I want. I dialled 999. I made myself tell you. I let them in. I'd always let them in. Your own daughter. Can you believe that? They have to be punished. I need to see them punished.

Rosemary Mrs Weston, I can't make any guarantees about what will ——

Mrs Weston But I love her. Annie. My little one. Always a smiler. Running round like a little smiley button. All that energy. Told me everything as happened in school, what the teachers said, what her friends done, everything. My others didn't. But Annie — I knew her. I knew what she thought, I knew what she felt, I knew what she wished. I *knew* her, Rosemary, I could see her more clearly than I could see myself. When you have a child of your own, you'll know. You'll see her, too. When she met Clifford, she told me all about it. She even told me when they first slept together. How many daughters tell their mothers that? Eh? Did you?

Rosemary No.

Mrs Weston cries during the following

Mrs Weston I can still see her. She can't hide from me. I don't forget things. I know her. And yesterday I could see her. For Annie to do that. Of all people. When you become a mother, Rosemary, you'll know what it's like to love someone more than you know how to cope with. I love Annie more than I've ever loved anybody. Even Charlie, God bless. It's not fair, is it? How can it be fair? They need to be punished. They have to be — why should I suffer? Why is it me? What have I done? What have I done?

Rosemary Mrs Weston, I promise to do all that I can to help you.
Mrs Weston And what's that?
Rosemary They can't have spent the money yet. Today's Sunday,
    remember? They'll find it hard to explain why they've got six
    hundred pounds in the house.
Mrs Weston It'll be in that shed.
Rosemary On Clifford's allotment?

Pause

Mrs Weston Do you think they'll go to prison?
Rosemary I don't know. It's more important to think about how we
    can get the money back.
Mrs Weston Clifford would deserve to go to prison.
Rosemary I tell you what. You finish drying your eyes, then you
    go into the kitchen, and you make us a nice cup of tea. And while
    you're doing that, I'll radio the station and get them to ——

The doorbell rings

Mrs Weston (*nervously*) Who's that? Who is it?
Rosemary Are you expecting anyone?
Mrs Weston Nobody comes on a Sunday.
Rosemary Would you like me to answer it? Or do you think I'd
    frighten the neighbours?
Mrs Weston You answer it. Thank you, Rosemary.

Rosemary exits

We hear the front door open

Mrs Weston listens intently

Derek (*off, in an exaggerated Irish accent*) The top o' the marnin'
    to yer.
Rosemary (*off*) Derek?
Derek (*off, in his normal voice*) You still here, then?

Rosemary (*off*) What are you doing here?

Derek (*off*) I come to deliver you from evil.

Rosemary (*off*) Good God.

Derek (*off*) Correct. Well, are you going to let me in, or are you going to let the cold freeze me from this mortal coil?

Rosemary (*off*) Derek, there's a tricky situation here. If you come in, behave yourself — and talk properly.

Derek (*off*) I usually talk improperly, but for you, my *petit chou*, I shall make an exception.

Rosemary (*off*) Oh — come on in.

Derek (*off*) I bet you say that to all the boys.

Derek enters. He is a detective constable, around thirty

We hear Rosemary close the front door

Rosemary enters

Derek (*showing Mrs Weston his warrant card*) Good morning, good morning. Mrs Weston, I presume. DC Barber at your service.

Mrs Weston (*immediately taking to him*) Honoured, I'm sure.

Rosemary Careful, Mrs Weston — you'll make him even more big-headed than he is already.

Derek Mrs Weston, I am the tider of good bearings.

Mrs Weston Eh?

Derek I bring news that will warm the very hearts of your cockle. Do you have a cockle?

Mrs Weston Give over — I haven't seen a cockle in years.

Derek Come, come, Mrs Weston — as the Bishop said to you last Sunday. I bet you've driven a few boys wild in your time, eh?

Mrs Weston Get away with you. He's a bit cheeky, isn't he?

Derek A bit? A bit! Let me tell you, Mrs Weston-Super-Mare — I am the cheekiest cheeriest charmingest chappie, with the choicest, chirpingest chittering chat-up.

Mrs Weston You're like whatsisname — *The Good Old Days.*

Derek I am of course too young to recollect such a programme. Besides, we were too poor to have a television when I were a lad. We used to sit round a cardboard box with a photograph of Eamonn Andrews stuck on the front.

Mrs Weston Eamonn Andrews — I used to like him.

Derek Yes — so did my grandmother.

Mrs Weston You cheeky devil.

Derek I tell you what, Mrs Weston. Could you do me a great big favour?

Mrs Weston I think I'm too old for that, dearie.

Derek Smut! Smut! Smut! The profanities of today's geriatrics!

Mrs Weston (*loving it*) Geriatrics!

Derek Mrs Weston, I have driven here through a terrible howling gale. The wind has whistled woefully wound my wusty Wover. I am in dire need.

Mrs Weston (*laughing*) I can see that.

Derek Mrs Weston, I need the stimulus of — drugs.

Mrs Weston Drugs?

Derek In liquefied form. In short, Mrs W., I need a cup of tea.

Mrs Weston Oh, I see. Your wish is my command, I'm sure. (*Brusquely*) Rosemary?

Rosemary Eh?

Mrs Weston Tea?

Rosemary No, thank you.

Mrs Weston Suit yourself.

Mrs Weston exits, humming to herself

Rosemary What was all that about?

Derek What?

Rosemary Your Bernard Manning act.

Derek You certainly know how to wound a man, Rosie.

Rosemary Well?

Derek I just like to keep the punters happy, Rosie, keep the hunters pappy. Softens the blow.

Rosemary What blow?

Derek The invisible blow of tidings ill.

Rosemary I thought you said you had good news.

Derek Good news, bad news — what's the difference?

Rosemary Quite a lot, I'd have thought.

Derek Not in the news.

Rosemary Eh?

Derek Not in the teller. Only in the listener.

Rosemary My God, who are you? Roy Chubby Brown or Bertrand Russell?

Derek Have you cracked the case yet, Rosie?

Rosemary As you are well aware, Derek, my name is Rosemary.

Derek How have you got on with Mrs Weston?

Rosemary Not as well as you, obviously — but well enough.

Derek Good.

Rosemary I feel sorry for her.

Derek Sorry?

Rosemary Yes. Sorry. It means to be sympathetic towards, or to feel pity for.

Derek Why?

Rosemary She had six hundred pounds stolen from her by her daughter and son-in-law. Can you imagine that?

Derek That is what Mrs Weston told you, is it?

Rosemary Yes. Obviously.

Derek Rosie … Rosemary … I do not wish to blunt your capacity for human sympathy, empathy, homeopathy, or even psychopathy — but Mrs Weston has proffered the most profulgent porkies since Trickie Dickie formulated his non-operative statements.

Rosemary Can you translate that?

Derek Mrs Weston has spun you the longest line of bull, moonshine and self-delusion since the last party political broadcast. In short, she is a compulsive psychotic liar whose imagination is far stronger than her faltering grip on reality. She has sucked you in.

Rosemary What are you talking about? You weren't even here when she ——

Derek My dear Rosemary, the money is still in this house.

Pause

Rosemary God, I can't believe how stupid I've been. You know, I let her stop me going in the kitchen. I never even looked at the bloody caddy.

Derek Thank you, Nick Faldo. Do not berate yourself, Rosemary. The money has been removed from the tea caddy; examining that particular object would not have aided your investigation.

Rosemary So where is it, Sherlock?

Derek The money or the caddy?

Rosemary The money, obviously. Stop taking the piss.

Derek (*after considering a rejoinder but rejecting it*) The money is in a shoe box in the cupboard under the stairs. It was put there yesterday afternoon by Mrs Weston.

Rosemary Why?

Derek Who can probe the mysteries of the human psyche with the lance of certainty? Like all obsessives, she yearns for reassurance but fears predictability. Consequently, she moves it about a lot.

Rosemary What?

Derek (*imitating her*) The money, obviously. Sorry ... She regularly moves it from hiding place to another.

Rosemary I have been a gullible fool.

Derek Yes. But I don't blame you.

Rosemary Don't be so bloody patronizing.

Derek I mean it. It wasn't your fault. It's very hard to disbelieve someone you're talking to.

Rosemary I can't stand much more of this. Go on — tell me how you know about the shoe box.

Derek Ah yes, the shoe box. Yesterday afternoon, Mrs Weston moved her money from the aforesaid tea caddy to the aforesaid shoe box following the observation of her son-in-law, Mr Clifford Williams, that the tea caddy was positioned in a location that rendered it virtually inaccessible to someone of Mrs Weston's diminutive stature.

Rosemary Only I bet he didn't use those lah-di-dah-I've-got-a-philosophy-degree words.

Pause

Derek Well? Aren't you going to ask me?

Rosemary Ask you what?

Derek How I know.

Rosemary I thought you knew everything.

Derek Don't get sarky with me, young Rosie — I am in the process of saving you from landing yourself in the proverbial.

Rosemary Oh, yes?

Derek Oh, yes. Your very good friend, Sergeant Adolf Dawkins, who thinks Genghis Khan was a wet liberal, who believes people's human rights diminish in proportion to the darkening of the pigmentation of their skin, who feels women should be kept out the police force along with all other handicapped people, who has pictures of Benito Mussolini on ——

Rosemary Get to the bloody point.

Derek Who sent you to interview Mrs Weston?

Rosemary Sergeant Dawkins.

Derek Who thinks a pretty young thing like you should forget policing and get back home to her knitting?

No response

Come on — tell your Uncle Derek.

Rosemary (*in a sing-song little girl's voice*) Sergeant Dawkins, sir.

Derek Who knows all there is to know about Mrs Weston, because she's made a million and one complaints to the Police during the last hundred and thirty-seven years?

Rosemary Really?

Derek Must be a million and two, now. "As nutty as a fruitcake", according to the egregious Sergeant Dawkins, who thus revealed in his command of the English language the originality and subtlety that so permeate his character. In my experience, fruit-cakes are not actually particularly nutty.

Rosemary Sergeant Dawkins wanted me to make a fool of myself.

Derek Yes.

Rosemary Which I have done.

Derek Yes.

Rosemary But you came dashing along on your white charger to save me from a fate worse than death.

Derek Aren't I wonderful? And do you know, I'm not even on duty.

Rosemary So you went round to the daughter's this morning?

Derek No.

Rosemary Well, how did you find out ——

Derek *Facilement.* No point in unnecessary effort. I was coming off shift when I heard Gauleiter von Dawkins boasting about how he'd set you up. Mrs Weston has accused Mr Clifford Williams of stealing her money — or, more regularly and more heinously, of *thinking* of stealing her money — many times before. I rang Mr Clifford, and he informed me of the transfer to the shoe box.

Rosemary But not Annie?

Derek Eh? No — Clifford just happened to answer when I phoned.

Rosemary No. What I meant was, she hadn't accused Annie before. This is the first ——

Mrs Weston enters, pushing a tea trolley with tea things on it. During the following she sits and pours tea for all three of them

Mrs Weston Here we are.

Derek Mrs Weston! Choccy biccies on a Sunday morning! How delightfully wicked — or wickedly delightful. I said you were a naughty girl, didn't I?

Mrs Weston I don't often have someone to make tea for.

Derek (*drinking his tea noisily*) Mmm. Delicious. Delicious. Do you know, I have not had a cup of tea to compare with this since — ooh, since nine o'clock this morning in the police canteen.

Mrs Weston You cheeky monkey. That's my best PG. (*She pauses slightly*) Suits you then, doesn't it, if you're a monkey? (*She chortles*)

Derek Oh yes — the adverts. They're awfully good, aren't they? I don't know how they get those chimpanzees to talk. My favourite is the one where they're playing with their balls.

Mrs Weston Don't think as I've seen that one.

Derek You must have. They go into the park, get their balls out, and start kicking them around all over the place.

Mrs Weston You need taking in hand, you do.

Derek Do you think Rosemary would do that for me?

Mrs Weston A nice young girl would do you the power of good.
If you was married, you'd weigh a few pounds less and you
wouldn't be so cheeky.

Derek A few pounds less! I'll have you know I have a very fine
figure. A very fine figure six.

Mrs Weston Mind you, you never will be, will you? Married. Boys
are more of your line, aren't they?

Pause. Mrs Weston has taken the wind out of Derek's sails

Rosemary (*trying to minimize embarrassment*) Mrs Weston, DC
Barber has some good news for you.

Mrs Weston Oh, yes?

Rosemary About your money.

Mrs Weston What about it? (*To Derek*) What's the matter, cat got
your tongue?

Derek (*trying to get going again*) Mrs Weston, I have a very bad
memory.

Mrs Weston Do you?

Derek Yes. It's so bad I went to the doctor's about it.

Mrs Weston Did you really?

Derek Trouble was, when I got there I forgot why I'd gone.

There is a slight pause. It was not a very funny joke

Mrs Weston Are you trying to say as I've got a bad memory?

Derek Do you ever — move your money about?

Mrs Weston That would be a stupid thing to do.

Rosemary Why?

Mrs Weston I'd forget where it was, wouldn't I? (*She pauses
slightly*) Here, what is this? What's going on?

Rosemary DC Barber talked to Clifford this morning.

Mrs Weston Clifford!

Rosemary Your son-in-law.

Mrs Weston I know who he is. What story did he spin you?

Derek He told me that from time to time you put your money in different hiding places. He said that yesterday afternoon you put it in a shoe box in the cupboard under the stairs.

A slight pause

Mrs Weston It'd be a bit big, wouldn't it?

Rosemary The cupboard?

Mrs Weston No, the shoe box, stupid.

Derek "You don't need a shoe box to keep five hundred pounds in." He said those were his very words to you yesterday.

Mrs Weston Five hundred pounds?

Derek All in notes, he said. Doesn't take up much space ——

Rosemary Mrs Weston had six hundred pounds.

Derek Sergeant Dawkins said you reported five hundred pounds as having been stolen.

Mrs Weston I never did. He's a liar.

Pause

Derek Well … I must have made a mistake.

Mrs Weston And I never moved it to no shoe box, neither. What's going on?

Rosemary We are trying to help you find your money, Mrs Weston.

Mrs Weston I've kept it in that tea caddy since … Oh, ages now. Before that I used to keep it — somewhere else. But that was years ago. I've always used that caddy, ever since I had it. Never put no tea in it.

Derek Would you mind if we had a look?

Mrs Weston What?

Derek In the cupboard under the stairs. Just to make sure.

Mrs Weston I never put no shoe box there. I never moved no money.

Derek Clifford told me you said you were putting the money there so that you wouldn't have to keep asking him to lift it down.

Mrs Weston I don't never ask Clifford to lift it down. *(She pauses slightly)* Only the once. He's as idle as a slab of lard. This is all lies. What are you doing to me?

Derek Mrs Weston, we just want to help you. Look. To put all our minds at rest, shall I go and have a look in your cupboard and see if the money is there?

Mrs Weston I never put no money there. I don't forget things.

Derek Let's just have a look, eh? *(To Rosemary)* Stay with her. It'll only take a minute.

Derek leaves the room

There is a pause

Mrs Weston Clifford'll be at the bottom of this.

Rosemary At the bottom of what, Mrs Weston?

Mrs Weston All this. The lies. The plotting against me.

Rosemary I don't think that anyone is plotting ——

Mrs Weston Annie would never have thought of this. She'd tag along, for Clifford's sake. But she'd not plot.

Rosemary Mrs Weston, let's just wait until DC Barber ——

Mrs Weston You never stop knowing your kids. But I know Annie more than ... more than I know myself. And I don't forget things. I remember. Across all the years. You know what I remember most about Annie?

Rosemary No, I don't.

Mrs Weston Shall I tell you? You want me to?

Rosemary Yes. Tell me.

During the following speech, Derek returns with a shoe box

Mrs Weston When Annie was nine. She was in Mrs Griffiths' class. A real Tartar, she was. The type of teacher you don't see nowadays. Scared all the kids stiff. They had this Maths test. On a Friday morning. I think they had a Maths test every Friday. This particular time, Annie was dead worried. She'd been off poorly for a few days and had missed most of the work. She was hardly ever off. I made mine go, snuffles or not. When she took the test that morning she was so scared of doing bad that she copied off the girl she sat next to. Mrs Griffiths — Gorgon Griffiths, they called her — never noticed a thing. At the end of the day Annie came bursting into the house, running as fast as her spindly legs would carry her. Her lungs were bursting, her eyes were flooded with tears. She flung herself at me, and told me over and over how she'd done something really terrible and she'd never go to heaven and Jesus had seen her doing it. She was a titchy girl, thin with long arms and legs and a little body. She clung on to me like a spider. That's what I remember. Like a spider. She was so upset and so ashamed, and could hardly get the words out. But she told me everything. We had no secrets. I could see her. I knew all her worries, all her feelings, all her hopes. That day, when she clung on to me like a spider, she was gasping for breath, she was sobbing her eyes out, she was more upset than I'd ever known her. But I didn't want it to end, I wanted it to go on for ever and ever.

There is a slight pause. Derek coughs slightly. There is no response from Mrs Weston

Rosemary (*taking the initiative*) Mrs Weston, DC Barber has found the box.

Derek Would you like me to open it, Mrs Weston?

Mrs Weston They're lying. I never moved no money. I don't forget things. I'm not like Mrs Harris. She's senile. And Clifford's poor old mother is in hospital. That place did for his dad. Rosemary — you understand me, don't you?

Rosemary (*politely, even though her attitude has changed*) Yes, Mrs Weston. I understand you.

Mrs Weston You open it, Rosemary.

Rosemary opens the shoe box. She looks inside, and then tips bundles of notes on to the table

Rosemary Well.

Pause

Mrs Weston This ain't right. Clifford's done this. Why should I want to move it? They're trying to send me round the bend. They've got it in for me. I don't know why. I never done them no harm.

Derek Mrs Weston. Listen to me. There is absolutely nothing wrong in forgetting something. We all do.

Mrs Weston I don't forget things. I never do. Sometimes I wish as I could forget things. But I don't.

Derek (*kindly*) It's not necessarily anything to do with getting old.

Despite Derek's kindly manner, this remark does not go down well

A memory can easily slip to the back of your mind. Then suddenly, the next day, there it is, right at the front again. Tomorrow — or Tuesday — this will all come back to you. (*She pauses slightly; then, to Rosemary*) I'll slip off now. Gerry will be wondering where I am.

Rosemary Who's Gerry? Your flatmate?

Derek He usually has something hot waiting for me when I get home.

During the following, Mrs Weston counts her money. She does so very professionally, like a bank teller. She counts it three times, each time more quickly, with a mounting agitation that is clearly evident

Rosemary I'll stay with her a little while. Make sure she's all right.

Derek prepares to leave; he and Rosemary move away from Mrs Weston

Derek As you wish. But you're not a social worker. You're a female policeman, as Dawkins would say. And she is a tough old bird.

Rosemary "A tough old bird" — a bit of a cliché for Mr Silvertongue?

Derek I occasionally lower myself to proletarian hackneyed unoriginality, in order to be understood by those of meaner intellect.

Rosemary Always the glib answer.

Derek Always the clever answer.

Rosemary Derek — I know you're a right clever dick. But thank you.

Derek Is that a compliment or an insult?

Rosemary You put yourself out ——

Derek As I always do …

Rosemary — and you've stopped me looking a right berk at the nick.

Derek Hold on — I can't achieve the impossible. But I am always glad to be proved right. And you're not a bad kid.

Rosemary Kid! And how old are you, Grandad?

Derek Old in wisdom, young in years.

Mrs Weston suddenly stops counting and stares blankly ahead of her

(*In a Humphrey Bogart voice*) I'll see you around, sweetheart. (*To Mrs Weston*) Goodbye, Mrs Weston.

No reply. There is a slight pause

Don't worry. She'll get over it. See you.

Rosemary See you.

Derek exits

We hear the front door open and close

Rosemary (*moving closer to Mrs Weston*) Mrs Weston … Mrs Weston? … Can you hear me?

Mrs Weston Of course I can hear you.

Rosemary I'm sorry … This must all seem very bewildering.

Mrs Weston Happen it is.

Rosemary If you tell me the name of your doctor, I could give him a ring and ——

Mrs Weston On a Sunday? I don't want no doctor.

Rosemary Is there anything I can get you? Would you like a fresh cup of tea?

Mrs Weston Rosemary. If I ask you a question, will you answer truthfully?

Rosemary I'll try to.

Mrs Weston (*snappily*) Trying's not enough.

Rosemary I will. I will.

Mrs Weston Do you trust him?

Rosemary Who?

Mrs Weston That pooftah.

Rosemary DC Barber?

Mrs Weston Yes. Him.

Rosemary Of course I do.

Mrs Weston Why?

Rosemary I don't know. Because I know him.

Mrs Weston Is he an honest man?

Rosemary Yes. Why are you asking me all these ——

Mrs Weston Listen to me, Rosemary. Listen to me very carefully. In front of me, on this table, is four hundred pound.

Rosemary Four hundred? But ——

Mrs Weston Yesterday, I had six hundred pound. And the day before that I had six hundred pound. I've counted my money hundreds of times. I could count it without looking at it. I know the feel of each note. Hundred and twenty in fivers, hundred and eighty in tenners, three hundred in twenties. Six hundred pound. And now there is four hundred. It has been very clever. Extremely clever. Eighty in fivers, hundred in tenners, two hundred and twenty in twenties. There is two hundred pound missing. There are two people in this world could have took it.

Rosemary Mrs Weston, are you sure ——?

Mrs Weston One of them is my daughter's husband Clifford. I don't forget things. I remember things. I never moved no money yesterday. But Clifford did. And when he did, he took two hundred pound. Now isn't that clever? He doesn't take the whole lot. He gets people thinking I'm old and doddery and forget things. So maybe you'll start thinking, she's forgotten she moved the money, so perhaps she's forgotten how much money she had in the first place. That is very clever. So now Clifford has two hundred pound to spend on that allotment.

Rosemary Mrs Weston, I can't really believe ——

Mrs Weston Can't you? I'm sorry about that, Rosemary. Because in that case it must have been your little friend Derek. AC/DC Derek. He was the one who fetched the money from the cupboard, wasn't he? If he slipped some notes in his pocket they wouldn't show. And he's clever. Keeps on letting you know how clever he is. He said I'd told that fat sergeant I'd had five hundred took. But I know I said six hundred. Spreading doubt, you see.

Rosemary Mrs Weston, I simply do not think that Derek ——

Mrs Weston Don't you? Think harder, Rosemary. I didn't think my Tony would go to Australia. I didn't think my Annie would marry a waster like Clifford. I didn't think a man would land on the Moon. I didn't think I'd lose two hundred pound.

Rosemary Derek would never steal money. You shouldn't accuse someone who came here to help you find ——

Mrs Weston He came to help you, dearie, not me. Still, I'm glad to hear what you say. Very glad. Because that means you think it was Clifford.

Rosemary I didn't say anything ——

Mrs Weston I hope it was Clifford. I'd like to see him arrested. I'd like to see him rot in gaol. I'd like to see him get beaten up by the warders. Screws, they call them. I'd like to see him get more and more desperate, more and more lonely, wishing all the time he was with Annie. So then he'd know. He'd *know* all right.

Rosemary Being vindictive is not going to ——

Mrs Weston The way he sits there, spilling tea on his jumper. And looking bored. He never looks at me. He always looks to the side. He looks fed up, as though I'm to blame. He's the one who ruined Annie. He took her. He ruined her. She don't hardly ever talk to me now.

Rosemary Forgive me, Mrs Weston, but I must be getting back to the station.

Mrs Weston What about my two hundred pound?

Rosemary I'll report back to Sergeant Dawkins, and he'll decide what to do.

Mrs Weston Will he?

Rosemary We shall probably continue with our enquiries.

Mrs Weston For two hundred pound? That's what's so clever. If all of it had gone missing, you'd have had to look for it. But two hundred — well, you just think I'm a cranky old bat.

Rosemary I have to be going, Mrs Weston. (*She pauses*) I shall see that this matter is pursued further, I promise you.

Mrs Weston Will you? Like Maureen promises to come and see me at Easter. Go on, Rosemary. You must be very busy. Get back to your station. Hurry off so you can escape from a demented old fool who has a crazy story about losing two hundred pound. She probably never had any money at all in the first place.

Rosemary That's not at all how I —— (*She pauses slightly*) I shall do the very best that I can, Mrs Weston, and I'm sure I'll see you again. I'll let myself out. Goodbye.

Rosemary leaves

We hear the front door open and close

There is a pause

Mrs Weston It is very clever. You have to admit that. She could be going straight round to his place. A hundred pound each. Not a bad day's work. She's not as innocent as she looks … That pooftah could be sharing it out with his boyfriend. They'll be laughing, in that loud way that queers laugh. Yet I quite liked him … I know it's Clifford. I can see him. He'll keep it all to himself. Not tell Annie nothing. She don't know nothing. My Annie would never have agreed to his dirty little scheme. He'll be down that allotment, chortling with his greasy mates. They've all got dirty fingernails … Hundred and twenty in fivers, hundred and eighty in tenners, three hundred in twenties. I had six hundred. I know I did. They won't crack me. I notice things. I remember things. I don't forget things. They won't win. I'll have them punished. They have to be punished. Hundred and twenty, hundred and eighty, three hundred … I shall find somewhere else for this. I'll hide it in … I won't even hide it in this house. I'll hide it in a secret place, where they'll never think of looking. They will look, but they shall not find. Ha. I'll watch them. I'll see them. They'll give themselves away. They won't crack me. They've got two hundred, but I know what's true. I had six hundred. They took it. But I'll get them. I notice things. I remember things. I don't forget things.

There is a pause. Mrs Weston sits still and in silence, looking determined

CURTAIN

FURNITURE AND PROPERTY LIST

Further furniture and dressing may be added at the director's discretion

On stage: Table
              Chairs

Off stage: Tea trolley with tea things on it (**Mrs Weston**)
              Shoe box full of banknotes (**Derek**)

Personal: **Rosemary**: notebook and pen

LIGHTING PLOT

Practical fittings required: nil

To open: General interior lighting

No cues

EFFECTS PLOT